South West C

NATIONA

WALKS ALONG THE
SOUTH WEST
COAST PATH

Ruth Luckhurst

ST IVES TO PADSTOW

COASTAL
PUBLISHING

A Coastal Publishing Limited Book

Editor Alison Moss
Design Jonathan Lewis
Production Peter Sills
South West Coast Path Project Manager Jo Kiddell

First published in 2013 by Coastal Publishing Limited
The Studio
Puddletown Road
Wareham
Dorset BH20 6AE

T: 01929 554195
E: enquiries@coastalpublishing.co.uk
www.coastalpublishing.co.uk

ISBN 978-1-907701-07-8

British Library Cataloguing-in-Publication Data
A catalogue record for this book is available from the British Library.

In the interests of your personal safety and enjoyment of these coastal walks,
Coastal Publishing Limited and the South West Coast Path Team recommend that
you follow fully the relevant safety advice in this book and The Countryside Code.
The South West Coast Path Team and Coastal Publishing Limited can
accept no liability whatsoever.

Printed and bound in Great Britain.

Front cover image: David Carvey.

With great thanks to the South West Coast Path Team's partners, who help to maintain and
manage the Coast Path, for providing pictures and contributing to the research for this book.
In particular, we'd like to thank the Cornwall Area of Outstanding Natural Beauty (AONB),
the National Trust and Natural England, as well as all the wonderful photographers who have
supplied their pictures for use in this book.

South West Coast Path

NATIONAL TRAIL

The European Agricultural Fund for Rural Development: Europe investing in rural areas

Image Acknowledgements
(key: t:top, m:middle, b:bottom, l:left, r:right, c:centre)
Images in this book are copyright of the photographers and artists.

All Aerial photographs © Coastal Publishing Limited; Front cover:
David Carvey www.themagicofcornwall.com; Peter Allsop 28t;
Bob Berry 43t; John Bishop 38m; Nick Cockman 38t, 39tl; Beverley
Dunstan 24-25b; Catherine Illsley - www.cillsleyphotography.com
11m; Ruth Luckhurst 11b, 16, 17, 20t, 20m, 21m, 21b, 24t, 28m,
29b, 35t, 35, 42t, 49, 54t, 54b, 55, 58m, 58b, 59, 62t, 62m, 63t;
Mike Mayor 39tr; Zoe Newsam 42-43b; Liz Osbourne 5b; Mark
Owen/South West Coast Path 29; Andrew Ray 34t; Peter Reddick
11t; Jennifer Rowlandson 48m; Andrew Trenoweth 48t; Visit
Cornwall 63b; Robin Whalley 10t.

CONTENTS

Along this part of the North Cornish coast idyllic stretches of golden beaches draw families armed with buckets and spades to sunbathe in sheltered coves and shrimp in rock pools, tiptoeing into echoing caves and running races around the rock stacks. Huge clean breakers rolling in from the Atlantic encourage surfers from all over the world, with body boards, long boards, short boards, kiteboards, and windsurfing boards, trailing behind them a festive air of summer and sunshine, wetsuits dripping from balconies and windows when the evening air hushes to the sound of the sea and the wheeling gulls.

Strong winds blowing in from the sea throw the sand onto the hinterland, building dunes – small mounds on the fringe of the beach but ever-growing hillocks on the landscape behind – creating unusual habitats for a wealth of rare species and exposing the eroded rocks on the shoreline to the relentless pounding of the ocean. Powerful underwater currents drag the sand up the long river valleys drowned by rising sea levels after the last Ice Age, changing the shape of the estuaries with every tide, altering the course of human history as inland ports silt up and others are created.

At Hayle, the 'towans' (Cornish for sand dunes) were once host to the National Explosives Company; at Padstow, at the northern end, the sailors' dreaded Doom Bar was said to be the result of a mermaid's curse.

Public Transport

Most walks give information about the nearest car park. Information about public transport services for these walks can be found online at www.southwestcoastpath.com.

The Traveline South West website provides up-to-date information about all public transport links. Visit www.travelinesw.com or call 0781 200 22 33

SAFETY FIRST!

Rockfalls and mudslides are an ever-present hazard on this coast and you are most strongly advised to stay away from the base of the cliffs and the cliff top. See page 64 for more safety information.

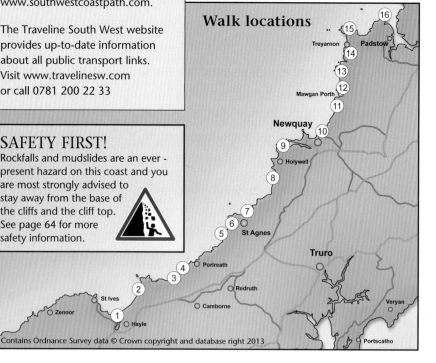

Walk locations

16
15
Treyarnon Padstow
14
13
12
Mawgan Porth
11
Newquay
10
9
Holywell
8
7
6
5 St Agnes
Truro
4 Porthreath
3
2
St Ives
Redruth
1
Zennor Camborne
Hayle
Veryan
Portscatho

Contains Ordnance Survey data © Crown copyright and database right 2013

In between, at Perranporth, the sixth-century oratory built by St Piran was buried in sand, as was the church his followers built to replace it. It was not until the eighteenth century that parishioners, tiring of having to dig their way into church, finally built the current church, well inland and still sand-free to date.

The rocks, too, make a major contribution to the breathtaking scenery of this Area of Outstanding Natural Beauty. The crashing waves have exploited every weakness in the cliffs and coves, resulting in spectacular stacks and arches, islands and headlands, caves and chasms.

For centuries, vast shoals of pilchards swimming into the bays provided the main livelihood for the people living on the coast, and fishermen worked in groups of three boats apiece to bring the fish inshore in their seine nets, directed to the shoal by the 'huer' onshore. The women and children worked in the pilchard cellars, packing salted fish into barrels and squeezing the oil from them. Eventually stocks of pilchards dwindled, and nowadays the diminutive fishing fleet's catch is crabs and lobsters for restaurants; which in turn have brought in the tourists. In 2003 Padstow restaurateur Rick Stein was awarded an OBE for his services to West Country tourism, while at nearby Watergate Bay, a charitable foundation created by fellow TV chef Jamie Oliver runs a beach restaurant dedicated to training disadvantaged youngsters to produce high-class meals from local ingredients.

Cornwall is rich in minerals, a result of the granite being forced up through the older rocks as continents collided, and these were laid down in deposits of copper, tin and tungsten, and later lead, silver, iron and zinc. Tin streaming has been carried out here for thousands of years, and later water power was harnessed to pump out water from the vertical shafts required to mine the veins of tin and copper. In the eighteenth and nineteenth centuries mining was big business in the region, and some of the country's best engineers worked at the cutting edge of technology to increase the efficiency of the steam machinery used in the engine houses.

When copper and tin prices collapsed due to increasing competition from around the world, one by one the mines closed, and today the many iconic engine houses and majestic chimneys stand in silent testimony to Cornwall's boom years. In 2006 select mining landscapes across Cornwall and west Devon were declared a UNESCO World Heritage Site in recognition of the huge contribution Cornish mining made to the development of global mining and modern society. For more information visit www.cornishmining.org.uk

West Pentire.

Gwithian
Towans

Phillack
Church

The Towans

TOWANS TRAIL

Hayle

Start/Finish P

Hayle
Swimming
Pool

Walk 1 – Towans Trail

Distance	6.5 miles (10.5km)
Estimated time	3 hours
Difficulty	•••••
Ascent	154ft (47m)
Map	OS Explorer Map 102
Starting point	SW 557377

Notes: Although fairly long, this is an easy walk with plenty of paths leading to the beach if you want to turn back earlier. In the eighteenth and nineteenth centuries Hayle was a key port and a major engineering centre, and the route through the sandy dunes passes the remains of the National Explosives Company, established in 1888. Hayle is one of the ten Cornish World Heritage Site areas.

From the car park by Hayle Swimming Pool turn right and follow the King George V Memorial Walk alongside the river, turning left on Black Road when you reach the end, and carry on uphill to Phillack Church. Go through the churchyard and turn left onto the path on the far side which heads towards the sea. When you come to the South West Coast Path turn right and continue through the dunes to the car park at Gwithian Towans.

If the tide is high, make your way back across the dunes to Hayle, but otherwise go down onto the beach and turn left, to head back along the famous golden sands. Turn left beyond the lifeguard hut, just before Black Cliff, and carry on along the path above the beach, all the way to the mouth of the estuary. When the path curves inland and turns onto North Quay carry on alongside the estuary and above the harbour to return to the car park.

WALK 1

Castle Giver Cove

The Knavocks

Godrevy Farm

GODREVY HEAD

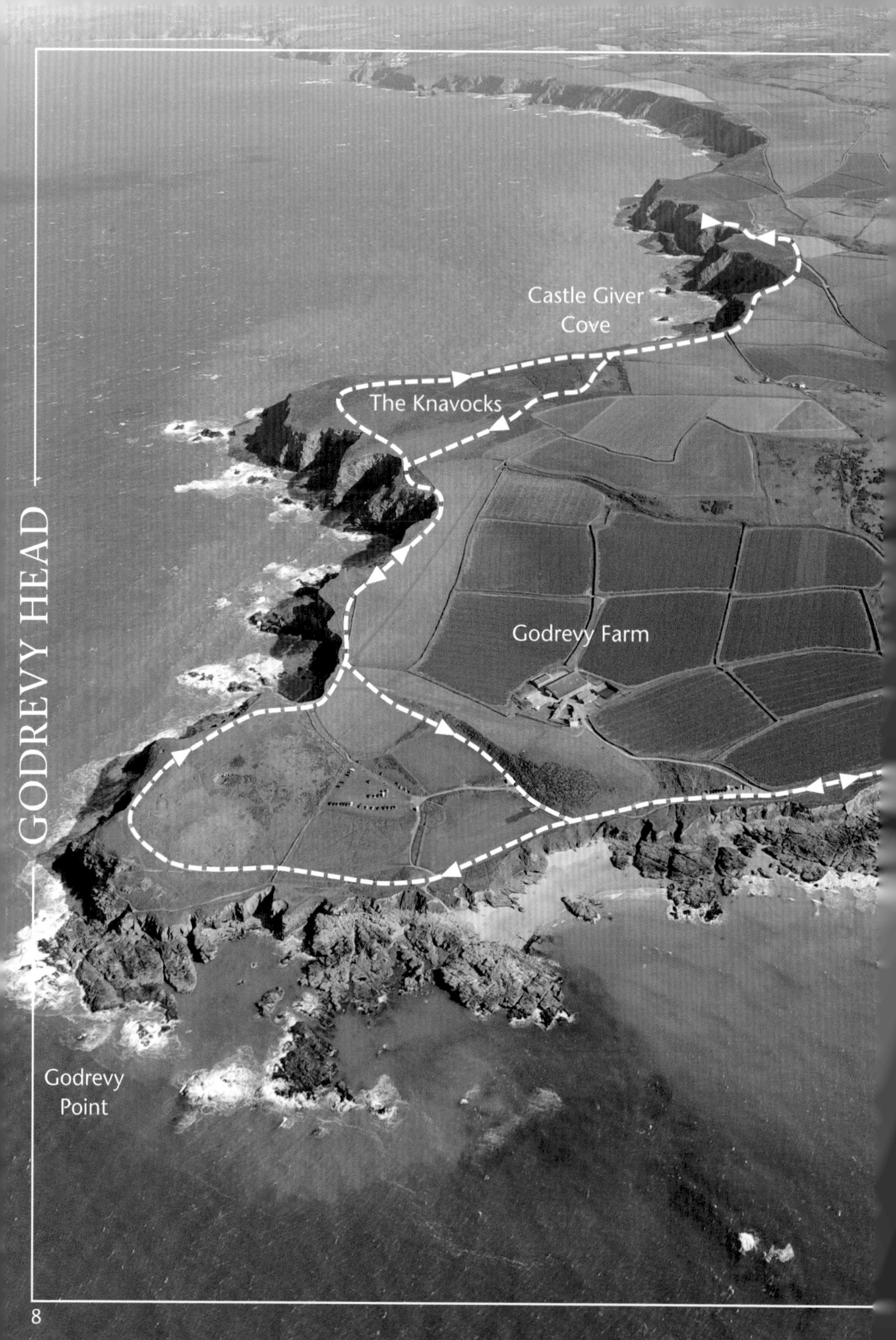

Godrevy Point

Walk 2 – Godrevy Head

Distance	3.75 miles (6km)
Estimated time	2 Hours
Difficulty	●● ● ● ●
Ascent	443ft (135m)
Map	OS Explorer Map 102
Starting point	SW 584423

Notes: An undemanding stroll with no major ascent or descent, with terrific views across St Ives Bay. In summer the maritime grassland is decked with clumps of wildflowers – thrift, sea campion, sheep's bit – and the cliffs are spiked with samphire plants and home to many nesting seabirds, including guillemots, razorbills, fulmar and cormorant.

From the National Trust car park at Gwithian take the path towards Godrevy to pick up the South West Coast Path and follow it above the sea towards Godrevy Point. The lighthouse on the Godrevy Island was built in 1858–59 after the SS Nile was lost with all hands. It is said to have been the inspiration for Virginia Woolf's novel To the Lighthouse.

Follow the path around Godrevy Head, past a tiny beach where seals are often spotted. Ignoring the path inland, carry on through the National Trust land at The Knavocks, with an optional detour around the headland itself. Coming through the gate on the far side, continue along the Coast Path until you reach the footpath heading inland, above Castle Giver Cove. Turn right and follow it over the Knavocks, back to the Coast Path on the far side of the headland. Turn left and retrace your steps to take the footpath on your left, cutting across Godrevy Head, turning left again on the Coast Path to return to the car park.

WALK 2

Godrevy Rocks, St Ives Bay.

During the late eighteenth and nineteenth centuries Hayle developed into a key industrial centre and shipping port, and now forms part of the Cornish Mining World Heritage Site. At its western extent was Harvey and Company, a pioneering engineering works, which produced the largest steam pumping engines ever made. The Harvey's name was to become a global brand with its engines installed in mines the world over. The company employed two Cornish inventors, Richard Trevithick and William West, both John Harvey's sons-in-law, whose efforts contributed greatly to its success. Among Trevithick's innovations were the Cornish Boiler and the first practical application of high-pressure steam in what would become known as the Cornish Engine. Trevithick, a prolific inventor, also designed a screw propeller for ships and in 1801 constructed the first practical steam road vehicle, the 'Puffing Devil', which was the precursor of all future steam locomotives.

Although the tower of Phillack Church dates back to the thirteenth century, most of the building is from Victorian times. The chi-rho Christian symbol in the gable over the south porch, however, betrays much earlier origins. One of only three in Cornwall, the motif was used predominantly in Gaulish and Mediterranean lands in the fourth and fifth centuries. Phillack as a holy site is linked with the Irish missionary St Pia Ia, also known as St Ia of St Ives, who arrived in the bay in the sixth century with her brother St Gwinear. It is believed that there would originally have been a wooden oratory, replaced with a stone chapel around AD 700.

About a mile along the Coast Path from where you join it at Phillack, and a little to the east, are Upton Towans. Known locally as 'Dynamite Towans', this area was the site of the National Explosives Company. Established in 1888 to produce dynamite for use in mines and quarries, the factory covered 300 acres of the Towans and by 1890 was producing 3 tons of explosives each day. During the First World War the company employed about 1,500 people, manufacturing up to 2,000 tons of cordite, gelatine, nitro-glycerine and gelignite for the British army and navy by the end of hostilities. The works closed in 1919, but were still used to store explosives until the 1960s.

Godrevy Lighthouse.

The Mexico Towans to Gwithian Towans Site of Special Scientific Interest (SSSI) covers Cornwall's second largest dune system, the north-west facing dunes of which are exposed to the full force of Atlantic gales. The continual shifting of the sands exposes the rocks to the north, eroded to cliffs, caves, stacks and arches, and remnants of former dunes are preserved on the sea stacks, making it an important area in the demonstration of the relationship between the dunes and the surface below them.

Breakers at Gwithian.

The sand is derived from crushed seashells, rich in calcium, and supports a wide range of plants and animals, while the past industrial and agricultural use of the land has created additional habitats. A fifth of all the plants to be found in Cornwall can be seen on the Towans, attracting many butterflies and moths, including some rare species.

On the Knavocks, Shetland ponies have been introduced by the National Trust to control the gorse and scrub with their grazing, and the coastal heathland is also home to many species of butterflies and birds, including ground-nesting stonechats with their black heads and orange breasts.

Summer flowers and stormy seas.

WALK 2

Start/Finish

P Tehidy

North Cliff Plantation

Reskajeage Downs

Basset's Cove

Hudder Down

Hell's Mouth

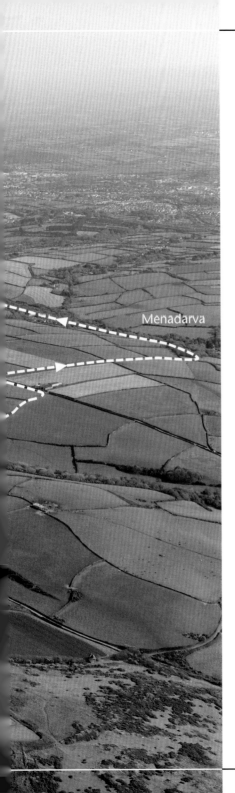

Menadarva

Walk 3 – Reskajeage and Tehidy

Distance	7 miles (11.25km)
Estimated time	3½ hours
Difficulty	● ● ● ● ●
Ascent	810ft (247m)
Map	OS Explorer Map 102/104
Starting point	SW 640439

Notes: A long walk starting high above plunging cliffs that tower over tiny caves and curving inland along Red River Valley, a tranquil haven for wildlife.

From the coastal car park above Basset's Cove, facing the sea, turn left on the South West Coast Path over Reskajeage Downs. Passing three car parks, carry on to round the small headland at Hudder Down. When the Coast Path meets the road above Hell's Mouth, cross the road and take the footpath immediately opposite. Follow it around fields to another road and turn left to take a footpath right shortly afterwards, through more fields and downhill to the buildings at Menadarva.

Drop down to the road, turn left and pick up the bridleway on your right just beyond, crossing the Red River to walk beside it through the Nature Reserve to come out by the caravan park. Turn left on the road and left again at the junction, taking the footpath on your right as the road bears left. Entering Tehidy on the Mineral Tramways Trail along West Drive, follow the yellow waymarkers, turning left at Otter Bridge and right at Kennels Cottage. Leave the yellow trail soon afterwards to turn left and follow pink waymarkers to North Cliff Plantation, carrying on ahead at the crossroads to come out at the car park by the road. Turn right up the track opposite, back to the car park above the cliffs.

WALK 3

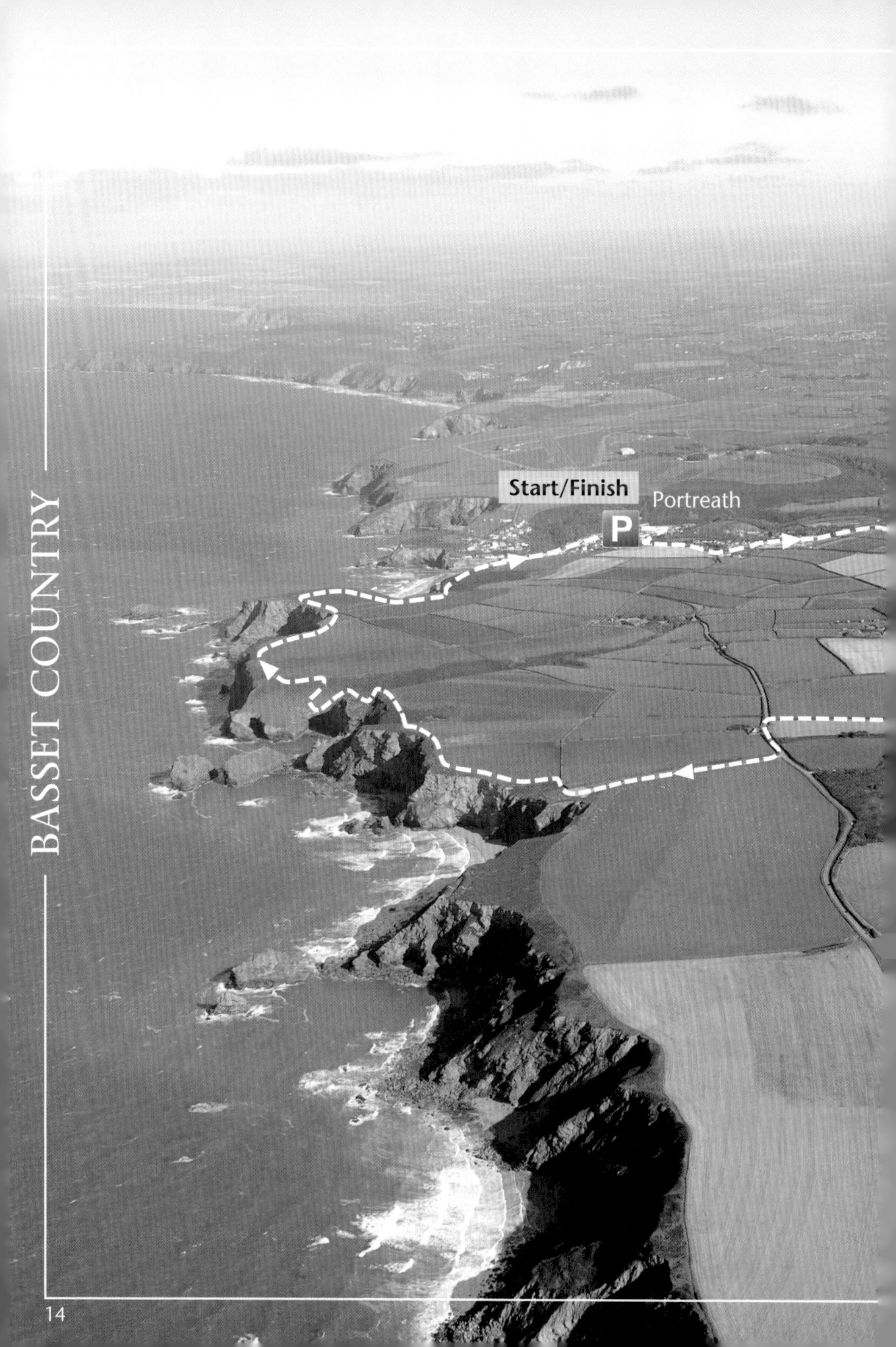

BASSET COUNTRY

Start/Finish

Portreath

P

Tehidy

Walk 4 – Basset Country

Distance	4.5 miles (7.25km)
Estimated time	2½ hours
Difficulty	●●●●●
Ascent	666ft (203m)
Map	OS Explorer Map 104
Starting point	SW 653453

Notes: A walk through the heart of one of Cornwall's most prosperous mining areas, featuring remnants of the mineral tramways and railways linking Portreath and Hayle to the district's mines and other industrial establishments. From Norman times much of the area was owned by the Basset family, whose country mansion was complemented by the landscaped grounds now managed by Cornwall Council as Tehidy Country Park.

From Portreath main car park cross the road, turning right to cross the stream and left at the Basset Arms car park entrance. Bear left along the footpath by the stream, along Tregea Terrace, continuing ahead at the junction to go under the bridge, which once carried the Portreath Incline of the Hayle Railway, and along Glenfeadon Terrace. At Primrose Terrace turn sharp right and bear right up the footpath, renovated as part of the Mineral Tramways Project and climbing steadily up a wooded side valley to zigzag around the Duchy Agricultural College farm buildings. Below the holiday lodges turn left then right up the track, keeping the lodges to the right.

Crossing the old Hayle Railway take the path ahead, crossing the road and carrying on by the car park to go into Tehidy. Follow the path through trees and along the Pine Walk by the

Tehidy woodland.

golf course. At the junction of paths bear left, following the pink trail along the edge of the woods to another junction by a clearing. Left here for the café and toilets and a view of the Bassets' Tehidy House, but otherwise follow the pink waymarkers ahead, turning right on the track opposite the gate and carrying on ahead along the pink and then blue trail to take the gate to the car park and the road beyond. Turn left and take the track right to the coast, turning right on the South West Coast Path to return to Portreath.

Located in one of Cornwall's most industrialised valleys during the peak mining period, the Red River Valley Local Nature Reserve is now a peaceful, partially wooded valley, with areas of heath and some lakes and ponds. Wildlife spotted in the reserve includes badgers, foxes, otters and woodpeckers, as well as an abundance of flowers and butterflies.

Most of the mineral extraction in the Red River Valley involved the recovery of tin, lost from mine dressing floors, and this form of tin streaming was still being carried out here in the 1960s. This has led to a much-altered river channel that lacks the slow and fast sequences present in a natural flow. In the past its banks have been strengthened using willow bundles and sometimes masonry.

At Bell Lake, the old millpond whose wheel powered the equipment used for tin streaming has been turned into a lake and wetland area, while a little further on, at Kieve Mill, the remains of the tin streaming works have been preserved. These include a concrete dressing mill, water channels, partially drained leats, and bases for the James's style tables that were used to shake the mineral slimes and extract the tin.

First recorded in the Domesday Book as Tedintone, Tehidy was the area's predominant manor, with lands extending through Redruth and Camborne as well as Illogan. From the twelfth century until 1916 it was owned by the Basset family, although the original manor house was sacked and rebuilt in 1493. It was demolished again in 1736–40 to make way for a Georgian gentleman's residence, built at a time when the family was enjoying high profits from its copper mines, and the extensive grounds were landscaped to complement it.

In 1780, Francis Basset marched his miners to Plymouth to strengthen the city's woefully inadequate fortifications, following an expected threat the previous year from the combined fleets of France and Spain, anchored off the coast. He was rewarded with a peerage, becoming Baron de Dunstanville. During his lifetime, 400 acres of Tehidy land were brought into cultivation as smallholdings by miners working in the flourishing copper mines, and the financing of the 1809 tramroad/plateway from Poldice to Portreath was also largely from his coffers.

His nephew, John Francis Basset, took over Tehidy in 1855 and set about revamping the mansion to make it one of Cornwall's finest buildings, with 40 bedrooms and a lavish drawing room with a gold ceiling.

Minerals, trams and railways

In the nineteenth century the Camborne and Redruth area was a major mining centre, producing half of Cornwall's metal output, and the ports at Portreath and Hayle were linked to a network of tramroads and rail routes running throughout the district. A tramroad, or plateway, was built along the valley bottom from Portreath to Poldice in 1809, greatly improving the transportation of ore and coal, and replacing the work previously done by many pack mules.

including the one down to Portreath Harbour from the hillside above.

This was followed by the construction of the Hayle Railway in 1837, connecting the town's engineering works and quays to the copper mines around Redruth and Camborne, to transport ore to the port and coal to the mines, with a branch to Portreath. It incorporated four cable-operated inclined planes on the steep sections, using stationary steam winders to raise and lower trucks on the slopes,

The Mineral Tramways Heritage Project was a £6 million regeneration initiative managed by Cornwall County Council. Closely following the old railway and tramway routes, 60 kilometres of paths have been created for walkers, cyclists and horse-riders, providing safe access to the carefully conserved remains of this unique mining area and using some innovative engineering techniques, including the use of recycled materials.

Chapel Porth

Wheal Charlotte

Walk 5 – Chapel Porth

Distance	3.5 miles (5.5km)
Estimated time	1½ hours
Difficulty	●●○○○
Ascent	430ft (131m)
Map	OS Explorer Map 104
Starting point	SW 692480

Notes: A short walk with some steep ascent and descent through a former mining area. Check out the tide times to catch Chapel Porth beach at low tide, when a long stretch of sand is exposed with fascinating rock formations and thriving rock pools, as well as sheer cliffs stained red and deep caves vividly streaked with multicoloured minerals.

From the car park at Porthtowan head towards the beach and pick up the South West Coast Path on the right, following it steeply uphill, or take one of the smaller paths zigzagging up the hill for a gentler ascent. At the top there is a further choice of paths. The Coast Path hugs the cliffs for the best sea views and a chance for birdwatchers to see the kittiwakes, skuas and gannets nesting below, while the inland route travels through the waste spoils around the disused copper mine of Wheal Charlotte. They converge above Chapel Porth and descend to the valley.

Staying this side of the stream, turn right onto the footpath and follow it up Chapel Combe, continuing ahead through the trees and merging onto the track joining from the left to come out on the road some distance beyond. Turn right and at the junction bear right onto the main road, passing the bridleway on the right to turn right again on Towan Road. Follow this downhill to the path above Porthtowan. Follow the path downhill, bearing right to return to the car park.

WALK 5

The Towanroath Shaft engine house at Wheal Coates, above the cliffs and caves at Chapel Porth.

Almost 300 million years ago, great heat and pressure was generated by continental collision, melting the Earth's crust to form granite, which was forced upwards through the slate. The separate masses of granite merged to form a long 'batholith', Cornwall's granite backbone. As a further result of the intense heat, water circulated through the fissures (cracks) in the granite, dissolving minerals from the rocks around them to form Cornwall's main tin, copper and tungsten deposits. About 50 million years later, further geological movements caused lead, silver, iron and zinc to form.

The cliffs towards the northern end of Chapel Porth beach are part of the rock bed exploited by the mine at Wheal Coates above, and the brightly coloured stains on the rock face are due to the minerals that were deposited in the rock. Minerals identified in Wheal Coates mine include pink and red copper and andalusite, yellow

Mineral stains at Chapel Porth.

and brown bismutite and cassiterite, blue and green bismite, glauconite and orthoclase, and blue and black schorl.

A local legend has a different explanation for the staining of the caves and cliffs on the beach. The giant Bolster fell in love with a girl named Agnes, who demanded that he prove his love for her by filling a small hole at the edge of the cliff with his blood. It looked like a very small hole, and Bolster readily agreed. However, it was a sea cave, and his blood drained out to sea, until he was so weak that he collapsed and fell to his death over the edge of the cliff, leaving the bloodstains in the cave to tell the tale. The story is re-enacted every May by locals using the site of the original St Agnes chapel. (See also Walk 6).

Sea caves are formed when the pounding of the ocean weakens and enlarges a fault in the rock. The water swirls around this, and the air pressure induced in the confined space continues to wear down the surface of the rock to create a cave. In time the pressure causes the roof to collapse, leaving a rock arch, like the ones that can be seen on the beach at Chapel Porth.

The dramatically veined red and green humps of rock to the left as you walk down onto the beach at Chapel Porth are further decorated by a colourful assortment of tenants. Crusted with tiny barnacles, the rocks are black with the crowded clusters of mussels of many sizes, with limpets dotted between them, and the snail-shells of a wide variety of whelks. Red sea anemones huddle in the dark corners where some water remains, being more vulnerable to drying out than shellfish. The rock pool environment is a very harsh one, in which the conditions are changing all the time and its residents need to be able to withstand the varying effects of tide and sunlight, including the changing temperature, oxygen levels and salt content of the water.

The path along the valley in Chapel Coombe is partially blocked by two banks of earth. These were the supports for a wooden bridge used in the Second World War by US troops stationed in a camp near

St Agnes Head. The circular area of raised bog by the bank is a 'buddle', a piece of equipment used to separate valuable minerals from waste (gangue) after the mined ore is crushed. Charlotte United engine house, visible ahead, was part of a group of mines here recorded as having produced 23,000 tons of copper ore.

The Wheal Ellen engine house near Porthtowan.

Ecosystem at Chapel Porth.

WALK 5

ST AGNES BEACON

St Agnes
Head

Trevaunance
Cove

St Agnes
Beacon

Chapel Porth

St Agnes

Start/Finish

Chapel Coombe

Walk 6 – St Agnes Beacon

Distance	6.25 miles (10.75km)
Estimated time	3¼ hours
Difficulty	● ● ● ● ●
Ascent	1020ft (311m)
Map	OS Explorer Map 104
Starting point	SW 719505

Notes: A long walk with some strenuous ascent and descent, this invigorating route climbs to St Agnes Beacon, an exposed area of heathland high above the surrounding area, giving great views in all directions. Between here and the coast are the remains of one of Cornwall's most extensive mining areas, one of the ten Cornish World Heritage Site Areas. It is now open land where bats live in the mine shafts and ravens and jackdaws inhabit the chimneys and engine houses.

From the car park in St Agnes walk down Trelawny Road to Vicarage Road. Turn right, carrying on past the Railway Inn to bear right along Goonvrea Road, turning right onto the clear-surfaced track at the top and right again on the lane to take the next track on the left. Keep to the middle track at the junction as you climb St Agnes Beacon. Go through the gate at the top and bear left at the fork to walk to the Ordnance Survey Trig Point.

Carry on ahead down the track towards the houses, forking right and then left, bearing right at the access track to a house. Turn left to cross the lane and follow the bridleway across another lane, carrying on along the track ahead. Bear left at the bottom and then right down a track into a field. Go through the gate and turn immediately right, following the path beside the stream, keeping right along the valley bottom at the fork. Turn left at the track and then left over a footbridge to go through a gate to a junction of paths. Turn right and walk through Chapel Coombe to Chapel Porth beach. Pick up the South West Coast Path up the access road on the right and follow the left-hand path around the cliff-tops, keeping left around St Agnes Head all the way to Trevaunance Cove.

Turn right to head inland along Quay Road, forking right up Stippy Stappy Lane and carrying on ahead through Churchtown to return to Trelawny Road.

The Towanroath Shaft engine house at Wheal Coates, above Chapel Porth.

At the end of Goonvrea Road on the left (and at other places along the walk) it is possible to see a large earthen bank, the remains of the ancient Bolster Bank. Although its date is not known, and there are speculations that it may have originated in the Bronze Age, it is thought more likely that it was built in the fifth or sixth centuries, at a time when Cornish landowners were under increasing pressure from Anglo-Saxon invaders heading west. It was once some 2 miles long and cut off a large area of the coast, including St Agnes Head and Beacon. In line with a tradition throughout Cornwall attributing unknown phenomena to giants, it was said to be the work of Giant Bolster, whose blood stains the cliffs below Wheal Coates (see Walk 5).

As with many other Cornish mines, the area around Wheal Coates was worked for

tin for centuries, but the iconic buildings on the cliff-top above Chapel Porth beach were not built until the 1870s. In 1881 Wheal Coates employed 138 people to mine and dress the tin, found in lodes just below sea level.

Three of the mine's buildings remain, stabilised and preserved in 1986 and maintained by the National Trust. The Towanroath Pumping Engine House of 1872 pumped water from the adjacent shaft, while the Stamps Engine House was added in 1880 to crush the ore. In 1910–13 a calciner was built to use heat to roast the ore and remove impurities, principally arsenic.

Wheal Coates.

Much of this walk passes through areas of heathland, characterised by gorse, thorn and bracken, with ling and bell heather growing beneath, as well as bristle bent grass. In spring there are pockets of primroses, bluebells and violets, while summer brings a blaze of colour on the coastal heathland from yellow bird's-foot trefoil and tormentil, pink thrift and white sea campion, as well as the purples and yellows of the heathers and gorse.

Coastal heathland is a scarce and declining habitat. In the UK some 85 per cent of heathlands have been lost in the past two centuries as a result of intensive agricultural practices. Bodies such as Natural England and the National Trust are working with landowners throughout the South West to reintroduce traditional methods of land management such as using grazing animals to reduce scrub and allow more delicate species to thrive.

Between 1632 and 1709, four unsuccessful attempts at building a harbour at Trevaunance Cove left the local lords of the manor deeply in debt. A fifth, built in 1710, was washed away within 20 years. It was not until 1798 that a harbour breakwater was finally constructed capable of withstanding the pounding waves.

The harbour was used to berth ships that supported the mines around St Agnes Head. Ore was dropped down a chute from the ore bins, still visible on the cliffs above, and coal was raised to the mines using a horse whim – a round platform supporting a winch drum turned by horsepower. The breakwater survived until the winter of 1915–16, when a great storm washed it away once again. Today only the granite blocks scattered around the cove remain as reminders of what was once a busy port.

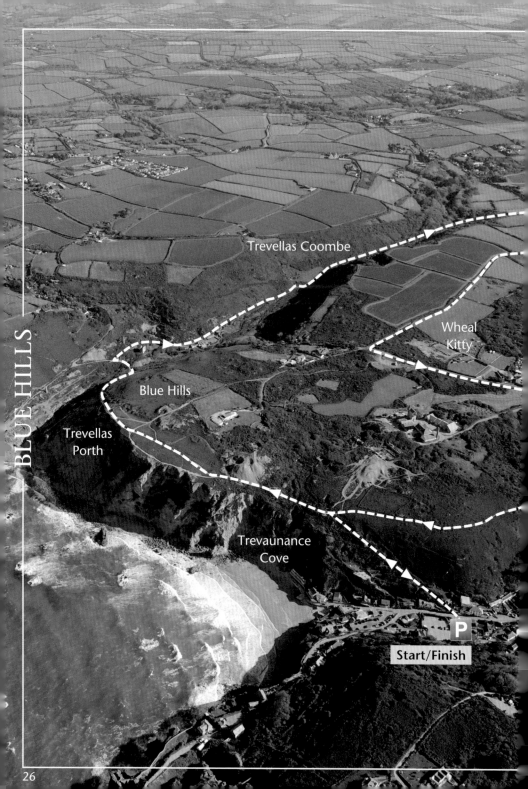

BLUE HILLS

Trevellas Coombe

Wheal Kitty

Blue Hills

Trevellas Porth

Trevaunance Cove

P

Start/Finish

Walk 7 – Blue Hills

Distance	3.25 miles (5.25km)
Estimated time	1¾ hours
Difficulty	●● ● ● ●
Ascent	289ft (88m)
Map	OS Explorer Map 104
Starting point	SW 721515

Notes: An easy walk, with some short stretches of gentle ascent and descent, through the Blue Hills tin streaming area, with optional detours to various industrial remains near a fascinating geology wall, and to Cornwall's only working tin producer.

From the car park above the beach at Trevaunance Cove turn right and head up Quay Road to pick up the South West Coast Path opposite Rocky Lane. Follow it uphill and around the cliffs above the beach to drop steeply down into the valley at Trevellas Porth. Turn left to follow the road at Jericho Valley and then take a path left for a detour to the beach and mining remains; otherwise turn right through the Blue Hills Tin entrance.

Carry on along the footpath through Trevellas Coombe towards Barkla Shop. Passing the footbridge, fork right uphill to the lane, and bear right on it to the road. Carry on ahead along the footpath opposite to the next road, then turn right, bearing right and crossing the road again to take the road opposite, past Wheal Kitty to another road. Turn left and walk to the main road at Peterville, turning right and right again onto Quay Road, taking the footpath marked up a rough lane to the right. This leads gently uphill above Quay Road and rejoins the Coast Path at the start of the walk. Turn left to return to the car park.

Trevaunance Cove.

For over a hundred years the Land's End Classic Trial has run through the steep lanes in Jericho Valley. Organised by the Motorcycling Club, the race is held every Easter. The original challenge, issued in 1908, was to ride from London to Land's End and back. Cars were admitted in 1914 and in 1920 the route became one-way only. Blue Hills had always been a particular feature of the event, and in 1936, with as many as 500 competitors taking part, the Club built the current road by enlarging an old miners' path.

Trevellas Porth Beach.

The small tin processing plant at Blue Hills Tin Streams is Cornwall's last tin works, producing tin from cassiterite gathered along the coastline. True tin streaming, or alluvial tin mining, was undertaken throughout Cornwall during the Bronze Age, possibly as long ago as 2,000 BC. Greek explorer Pytheas of Massalia, visiting Cornwall around 300 BC, remarked upon the cosmopolitan nature of its miners and other inhabitants, and their friendliness. At that time Cornish tin was taken by ship to France, where packhorses carried it to the ancient tin-trading port of Marseilles, from where it was distributed throughout the Mediterranean.

Mining was a dangerous occupation, and as always happens in difficult circumstances a sense of being in this together led to strong bonds, below ground and out in the wider community. In the late nineteenth century Lamp societies raised funds to install gas lighting, while charities such as the Dorcas Society provided clothes and bedding for the needy.

Like the workers in the Welsh coal mines, Cornish miners often sang as they worked underground. At the end of the shift, as they gathered at the shaft, waiting to be raised to the surface, a miner might begin to sing. Those around him would join in, and the song would be taken up by men on all levels throughout the mine, until the shaft rang with song. On the surface, too, in the pubs and in the churches they expressed themselves through music, and many communities had a formal male voice choir singing in full four-part harmony. In 1983 a festival of massed Cornish choirs filled the Albert Hall, giving rise to the formation of the Federation of Cornish Male Voice Choirs, which continues today.

The conical mesh caps which can be seen over some of the mine shafts, known as 'Clwyd Caps', were installed as a public safety measure.

Trevellas Coombe.

Elsewhere shafts are often secured with 'Bat Castles' to allow access for colonies of bats using these to roost.

If you visit the beach at Trevellas Porth, take a moment to look at the mining remains above the beach. The stone used in the walls displays a remarkable number of different rock types, with many fascinating features.

The Cornish Pasty

Ask anyone from over the Tamar to name just one Cornish delicacy, and the answer will be a resounding 'Cornish pasty' – granted protected status by the European Commission in 2011 and now only permitted to be called a Cornish pasty if it is made in Cornwall, and to the traditional recipe. The pasty evolved as the best way of feeding a hungry miner during his long hard shifts underground, and the definition of a good pasty was said to be one that would still be intact after a fall down a mineshaft. Made by filling a circle of pastry with diced beef, potato, onion and swede, and folding it over, often a pasty would also contain apple and jam at one end, to form a dessert.

St Piran's
Oratory

St Piran's
Church

ST PIRAN

Reen Sands

Perranporth

Hendravossen

St Piran's Round

P Start/Finish

Walk 8 – St Piran

Distance	5 miles (8km)
Estimated time	2¼ hours
Difficulty	● ● ● ○ ○
Ascent	417ft (127m)
Map	OS Explorer Map 104
Starting point	SW 779544

Notes: A fairly level walk exploring the traces of the fifth-century missionary, St Piran, said to have washed up on his millstone after he was banished from Ireland. There is limited parking at the start of the walk - please park considerately. If there are no spaces, park in Perranporth and start the walk from the beach instead.

From the layby at St Piran's Round follow the footpath to the right of the Round, turning left on the lane beyond and crossing the road to continue towards Hendravossen. Ignore the lane on the right and take the one on the left after it, turning right on the road. At the T-junction carry on ahead along the footpath and follow the waymarkers over the grassland, turning right on the path beyond to the remains of St Piran's Church and the medieval cross nearby.

Retracing your steps to where you joined this path, head towards the sea. With the modern cross to your left in the dunes, St Piran's Oratory is on your right. When you reach the South West Coast Path, turn left to follow it through the dunes to the beach at Perranporth. From there take the footpath inland, over Reen Sands to the main road at Tollgate. Turn left and then right at the right-hand bend, ignoring the lane on your left but taking the footpath on the left just after it. Follow the path to Rose, turning right on the road and then bearing left on the lane just after the junction, which will bring you back to St Piran's Round.

WALK 8

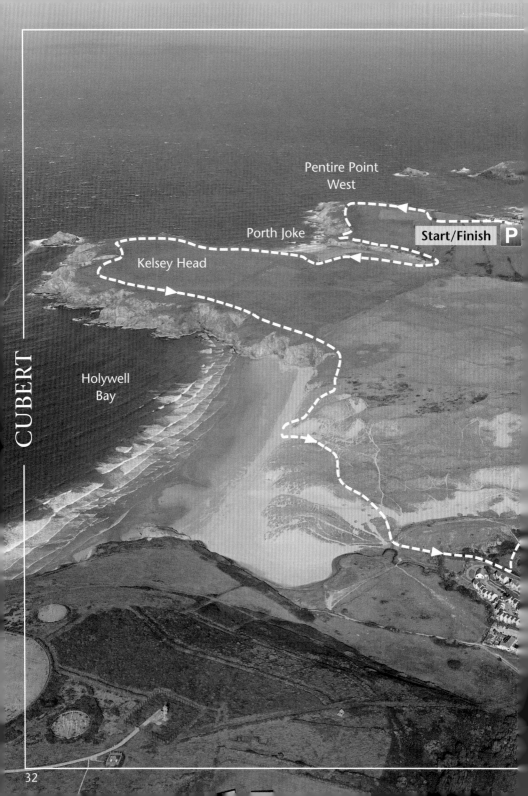

CUBERT

Pentire Point
West

Porth Joke

Kelsey Head

Holywell
Bay

Start/Finish P

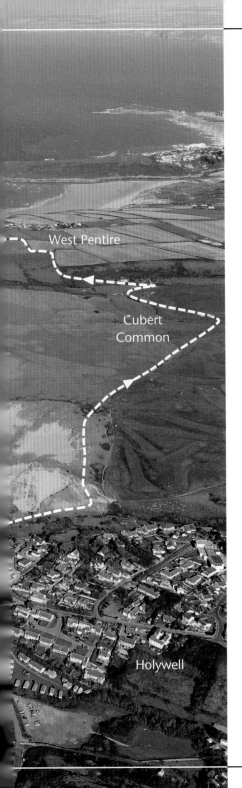

West Pentire

Cubert
Common

Holywell

Walk 9 – Cubert

Distance	4.5 miles (7.25km)
Estimated time	2¼ hours
Difficulty	●●●●●
Ascent	499ft (152m)
Map	OS Explorer Map 104
Starting point	SW 776606

Notes: An easy walk around two headlands, with an optional shortcut. The Cornish name for Porth Joke was 'Porth Lojowek', meaning 'plant-rich cove'. About 150 different species of plant thrive here today, and in the summer it is a riot of colour. The whole of Kelsey Head is a Site of Special Scientific Interest (SSSI) for the abundance of wildlife in its wide range of habitats, which include sand dunes, maritime grassland, wet meadows and brackish marsh.

From the West Pentire car park head for the coast, turning left and then right along the edge of a field. At the end take the left-hand path and then turn right to join the South West Coast Path. Turn left and follow it around Pentire Point West to Porth Joke. Take the footpath left for a shortcut, but otherwise cross the beach and continue on the Coast Path to Kelsey Head. Look out for fulmars nesting on the cliffs and buzzards inland. On the tip of the headland are the remains of an Iron Age cliff castle.

At Holywell follow the Coast Path inland from the beach, crossing the junction and heading downhill to a four-way junction, taking the left-hand path here. Continue ahead, turning left on the track and keeping right past the disused quarry. Just before Cubert Common take the next small path on the left, to follow the track uphill, past another disused quarry and around fields to return to the car park.

WALK 9

Early morning, Perranporth Beach.

Britain's highest sand dunes and Cornwall's largest dune system, Penhale Dunes, north of Perranporth, are thought to have been formed over 5,000 years ago, when changing sea levels caused sand to build up on a rocky plateau. They are a 'hindshore system' – a dune system exposed to onshore winds strong enough to drive large quantities of sand some distance inland in huge ridges which then become stabilised, leading to unusual communities of plants and insects.

The whole area is a SSSI for its wildlife. A wide diversity of plants provides food and shelter for large numbers of insects and invertebrates, which in turn attract mammals and many birds. Sparrowhawks and peregrine falcons hunt overhead, while wheatears and stonechats sing from the gorse and thorn bushes. Butterflies also flourish: the silver-studded blue, the small copper, the brown argus. Of especial note is a rare butterfly found in only two colonies in Cornwall, the grizzled skipper.

When St Piran's Oratory was buried in sand, around the ninth or tenth century, its congregation built a new church a little further inland, hoping to protect it from being similarly swamped. The oldest part of the old Perranzabuloe Parish Church is believed to be from the eleventh century and was recorded in the Domesday Book as Lanpiran ('St Piran's holy site'). In the twelfth century it was a collegiate church, and by the fourteenth century it had become a major centre for pilgrims travelling on the St James Way to Compostela in Spain.

Exacerbated by mining operations that drained the stream, shifting sands continued to be a problem, and by the eighteenth century parishioners often had to dig out the porch to gain entry to the church. Early in the nineteenth century, yet another church was built, this time inland on its present site in Perranzabuloe, and the old church in the dunes was abandoned to its fate.

The early medieval cross beside the ruined church is one of only two three-holed crosses in Cornwall. Recorded in a tenth century charter as the 'Cristel Mael', it is thought to be an ancient boundary marker.

St Piran's Round, or the Perran Round, was a medieval 'plain an gwarry' or amphitheatre, unique to Cornwall, where miracle plays were staged. The only other similar round remaining in the county is in St Just in Penwith.

Perranporth.

Conservation at Perran Sands includes grazing ponies.

St Piran

According to legend, St Piran built his first small chapel on Chapel Rock on Perranporth Beach, building the Oratory in its present position some time later, when he began to preach from here. Soon his 29-foot by 12-foot chapel was too small to accommodate his followers, and over the years the chapel was enlarged and improved a number of times. Archaeologists believe that there were other structures around the Oratory, and a sizeable graveyard. A small lake nearby prevented the building from being buried in sand; but this drained away in time, and the Oratory disappeared in wind-blown sand, although it kept a place in local legend.

Excavations carried out in the nineteenth century uncovered three skeletons under the floor, including a very large one minus its head. St Piran was said to be a very tall man, and after his death (at the age of 200, supposedly through falling down a well while drunk) his skull was kept in an iron-bound relicry.

NEWQUAY'S TWIN HEADLANDS

Newquay

Start/Finish **P**

Towan
Head

Fistral Beach

Lewinnick
Lodge

Pentire Point
East

Crantock Beach

Walk 10 – Newquay's Twin Headlands

Distance	7 miles (11.25km)
Estimated time	3¼ hours
Difficulty	●●●●○
Ascent	463ft (141m)
Map	OS Explorer Map 104
Starting point	SW 815619

Notes: A long walk with plenty of shortcuts, visiting the many facets of Newquay, including the fantastic sandy beaches and Atlantic breakers which make it one of Britain's surf capitals, as well as its rocky headlands with their panoramic views and the tranquil estuary where the River Gannel meets the sea.

From Newquay's railway station join Cliff Road, turning left to cross the road and bear right to join the South West Coast Path on the Tram Track. Continue along Bank Street and then Fore Street to North Quay Hill and the harbour. Follow the Coast Path waymarkers up the steps from the north side of the quay, past the Huer's Hut, and carry on around Towan Head to Fistral Beach, detouring to the tip of the headland for stunning coastal views.

Continue along the Coast Path to the end of Esplanade Road. Turn right and then right again to walk past Lewinnick Lodge and on to the end of Pentire Point East, the site of an Iron Age cliff castle. Rounding the point, follow the path on Riverside Avenue, bearing right along Pentire Crescent and Penmere Drive. Take the first right and follow the path to the river, turning left to continue upstream. Join Trevean Way keep bearing right to continue along Tregunnel Hill to Gannel Road. Turn right on the A392, left on Trenance Lane and left on

Crantock Beach

Trenance Road to continue ahead along Berry Road. Bear right onto Cliff Road to return to the station.

Newquay was once a bustling port. As well as the fishing boats working in threes to bring in the pilchards, the railway brought china clay and ore to be shipped from the harbour. By the end of the last century, however, the mines were closing and the pilchards no longer swam inshore in huge shoals. In their place the tourist industry took off with the railways bringing visitors, drawn by the spectacular coastline and the long sandy beaches.

In the early 1960s the rising numbers of bathers led to the growth of life-saving clubs on the South West's beaches, and combined with the Atlantic swell rolling in on the North Cornwall coast in high clean

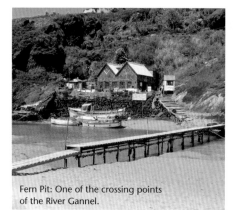
Fern Pit: One of the crossing points of the River Gannel.

breakers, this made it a popular venue for the surf culture which was spreading from America and Australia. Newquay became the capital of British surfing, a status it still claims today.

The Tram Track follows the line of an old horse-drawn tramway, built in 1849 and

Crantock Beach looking towards Newquay.

used until 1926 to carry ore to Newquay Harbour and to bring back coal and other supplies.

The mouth of the River Gannel was a thriving port until the end of the nineteenth century. Vessels brought their cargoes into Fern Pit, on the Newquay bank of the river – coal, fertiliser, limestone and earthenware – and the cargo was transferred to shallow-draught barges to catch the flood tide up to Trevemper, an important trading centre 3 miles upstream. Coal and limestone were also transported along Penpol Creek to a lime kiln at Pen Pol, where they were burned together to make lime, used as a fertiliser. Quays, steps, mooring rings and chains can still be seen along the wooded shoreline of Penpol Creek.

Pilchard fishing

The origin of the phrase 'raising a hue and cry': a huer was posted at a strategic place to look out for the massive shoals of pilchards arriving in late summer. When he spotted the silvery-red movement below the sea's surface, and the tell-tale diving seabirds, the huer would shout 'hevva' ('shoaling place'), and use a series of signals to tell the fishermen where to spread their seine nets. Once the fish were encircled by the seine this was towed ashore and a smaller 'tuck' net placed inside it to retrieve the fish, to be sent to the processing 'palas' ('place'), where they were packed into barrels between layers of salt and compressed. The oil was sold separately, although in some places it was used to power streetlamps instead.

The fishermen's wives would celebrate the arrival of the fish by baking Hevva Cake, using a scone-like mixture with dried fruit to represent the fish, baked in small rounds scored with a criss-cross pattern to represent the nets.

Trevarrian

Beacon
Cove

Griffin's
Point

Stem
Point

Stem
Cove

Tregurrian

P Start/Finish

Watergate Bay

Walk 11 – Tregurrian and Trevarrian

Distance	3 miles (4.75km)
Estimated time	1½ hours
Difficulty	●● ○ ○ ○
Ascent	417ft (127m)
Map	OS Explorer Map 106
Starting point	SW 842650

Notes: An easy stroll high above Watergate Bay, a popular surfing beach and 2 miles of golden sand when the tide is out. Turning inland at the hamlet of Trevarrian, the route returns across fields fringed with banks of ox-eye daisies and other wildflowers. The path may be muddy in places so good footwear is recommended.

From the car park at Watergate Bay take the road steeply uphill towards Trevarrian to pick up the South West Coast Path on your left. Follow the coastal path above the cliffs, around Stem Point, Stem Cove and Griffin's Point, once an Iron Age promontory fort. Dropping down towards Beacon Cove, leave the Coast Path to turn right inland towards Trevarrian. Carry on alongside the stream when a path joins from the right, following the road ahead into the village.

Take the footpath signed to your right, going through the small gate beside Wayclose and respecting the residents' privacy as requested, follow it straight ahead through two fields, exiting at the far end of the right-hand hedge of the second, to come out on a farm lane. Turn right on the road and walk to Trevarrian Hill. Turn left (watching out for traffic) to return to Watergate Bay.

WALK 11

There is a wide range of marine plants and animals at Watergate Beach, a result of the warm and cold currents that converge here. Above the high water mark, herring gulls and fulmars nest, and clumps of tufty pink thrift abound on the cliffs. You may be lucky enough to witness the high-speed dive of a peregrine falcon.

On the upper shore, sand hoppers and beach bugs known as sea slaters clean up the rotting seaweed, while on the middle shore below them – the rock pool zone exposed twice a day by the tides – molluscs such as limpets graze the miniature algae on the rocks. On the lower shore, only exposed during spring tides, creatures that are mainly aquatic have evolved to endure brief spells of exposure to the air. Look out for the shanny, an astonishing fish able to survive out of water. Out in the open sea beyond, the Gulf Stream brings in plankton, food for jellyfish, sun fish and sometimes even bottle nosed dolphins and basking sharks.

A number of fields around the footpath between Tregurrian and Trevarrian were referred to as 'Whitestone' in a tithe

Tregurrian daisies.

document of 1840, leading historians to believe that there may have been a standing stone here, from the Bronze Age, or possibly even from the Neolithic period, over 4,500 years ago, although there is no trace of one now. Located nearby are what are believed to be the remains of a more recent Romano-British and Iron Age round, dating from the same time as the promontory fort on Griffin's Point. The fort, with three ramparts once barricading it on the landward side, would have been used as a defensive site, taking advantage of the natural protection of the cliffs, while the round was a settlement, probably associated with it.

Watergate Bay from Stem Point.

Fifteen Cornwall

Every morning local farmers, fishermen and growers deliver fresh produce to Jamie Oliver's Fifteen Restaurant on Watergate Bay, where over 80 per cent of the food served is grown, reared or processed in Cornwall. Opening for breakfast at 8.30, the restaurant serves high-quality meals right up to midnight, with just a couple of short breaks during the day, and the menu is changed twice daily. Ingredients used in the restaurant include St Austell Bay mussels, Little Wheal cheese from Bude, Rodda's cream from Redruth, John Dory fish from St Ives, pasta made from Padstow wheat, eggs from traditional breeds of hen reared in Liskeard - even the seasalt comes from the Lizard peninsula.

What makes Fifteen Restaurant different is its staff. Part of a global social enterprise founded by TV chef Jamie Oliver, Fifteen Cornwall aims to 'empower those who deserve a second chance in life'. Every year the restaurant takes on a group of disadvantaged youngsters, aged 16–24, and trains them in the art of serving fine food to a discerning public.

The Cornwall Foundation of Promise is a registered charity and it promises to 'do everything in its power to help each [individual] to create the productive, successful life they'd like to achieve'.

Mawgan
Porth

Start/Finish P

Beacon
Cove

Berryl's
Point

St Mawgan

Trevarrian

Walk 12 – Mawgan Porth and St Mawgan

Distance	5.5 miles (8.75km)
Estimated time	2½ hours
Difficulty	•••••
Ascent	696ft (212m)
Map	OS Explorer Map 106
Starting point	SW 849673

Notes: A delightful walk along the valley heading inland to St Mawgan, passing the site of a noted settlement from the Dark Ages and a Tudor convent at Lanherne. The route returns on a path high above the marshes and ponds of the River Menalhyl's floodplain, taking the coastal path back to Mawgan Porth.

From the car park at Mawgan Porth walk up the road towards St Mawgan to pick up the bridleway on the left just before the road crosses the stream. Bear right along the footpath when others join from the left, and follow it through the trees and the field beyond, bearing right down the lane to carry on along the road ahead to the T-junction. Take the footpath opposite and follow it through the woods, turning right on the road to bear right through St Mawgan.

Turn right past the church and walk steeply uphill, past Lanherne, to take the second track on the right and follow the footpath through fields. Crossing the stream, climb through the fields beyond to cross the road and the field opposite, coming out on the main road into Trevarrian. Fork left through the village, crossing the road beyond to take the footpath opposite through fields to the South West Coast Path at Beacon Cove. Turn right on the Coast Path and follow it around Berryl's Point to drop into Mawgan Porth, turning left on the road to return to the car park.

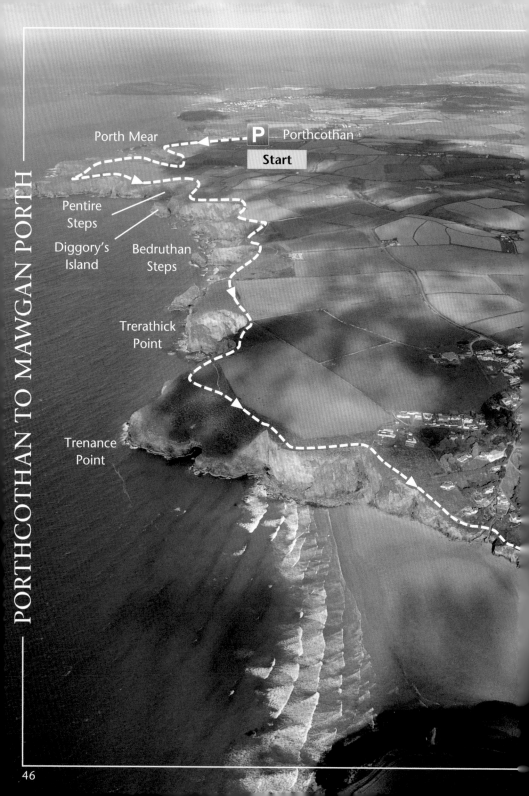

Porth Mear

P Porthcothan

Start

Pentire
Steps

Diggory's
Island

Bedruthan
Steps

Trerathick
Point

Trenance
Point

Mawgan Porth

Finish

Walk 13 – Porthcothan to Mawgan Porth

Distance	4.5 miles (7.25km)
Estimated time	2½ hours
Difficulty	● ● ● ○ ○
Ascent	623ft (190m)
Map	OS Explorer Map 106
Starting point	SW 858719

Notes: A high-level stroll along the coast to the ancient settlement of Mawgan Porth, passing some spectacular rock formations in the sandy coves between the cliffs and headlands of one of Cornwall's unspoilt gems. Take the bus back; or park in Mawgan Porth (SW849673) to catch the bus to Porthcothan and walk back.

From the car park in Porthcothan head towards the beach and pick up the South West Coast Path on your left to follow it above the beach, crossing the stream to round the headland to the cove at Porth Mear ('Great Cove'). Crossing another stream, carry on above the cliffs and headlands, across Park Head, around Pentire Steps and past Diggory's Island.

Continue on the Coast Path above the spectacular rocks and islands at Bedruthan Steps, passing the island at Pendarves Point to come to Whitestone Cove. At Carnewas Point the 'island' is still attached to the mainland by a narrow causeway of rock, visible at low tide. Carry on past the disused mineshaft at Trerathick Point, above two tiny coves far below, to Trenance Point, and descend gently towards the beach at Mawgan Porth. Stay with the Coast Path all the way to the road, turning left to the bus stop.

WALK 13

The cliffs at Porthcothan Bay.

Although it is best loved for the spectacular shapes of the islands, stacks and arches crowding the beaches around Bedruthan Steps, the geology for which the area is designated a SSSI is rather less obvious. The rocks are of particular importance for the fossils in the strata from the Eifelian Age, almost 400 million years ago. Notable among these is the Pteroconus mirus, a large planktonic creature which swam in the open seas and is believed to have had bladders to help it float. Other fossils found here include bivalves, some underwater scavengers similar to trilobites, the flat discs of a stalked sea lily known as a crinoid, and a primitive jawless fish known as a pteraspis.

The other SSSI feature at Bedruthan Steps is its plant population. Two unusual species found here are the tree mallow, with its pink and purple bell-shaped flowers, and the golden samphire, whose dandelion-like flowers sprout from clusters of leaves

Trevose Head Lighthouse.

resembling miniature green beans. These leaves are edible, and are often added raw to salads or boiled and served with butter like asparagus.

Like Chapel Porth, near St Agnes (Walk 5), and Port Quin, to the north of Padstow, the rocks on Porthcothan Beach, as well as having been eroded by the sea into dramatic cliffs and caves, are stained many colours by the minerals they contain. If you pass by at low tide, check out the caves on the left-hand side of the beach.

Like many of the headlands on this part of the Cornish coastline, in the Iron Age the tip of Park Head was a promontory fort, or cliff castle. Around the headland the cliffs have slumped: take care not to venture too close to the edge. Between the headland and the path are also stretches of tumbledown hedge bearing the herringbone pattern characteristic of North Cornwall, known as 'Jack and Jane' hedging or 'curzyway'.

On the hillside above the beach at Mawgan Porth are the remains of a Dark Age settlement dating from the late Saxon period, around AD 850–1050. The site was excavated in the middle of the last century, uncovering three courtyard house complexes, two of which are still visible in the landscape. The walls were faced with stone but built of soft slate and earth, and each building had a long room opening into a courtyard which was otherwise enclosed by smaller rooms. The long room was partitioned to accommodate livestock while still separating the animals from the central living area, which had a hearth and wall cupboards.

Lanherne

Lanherne is an ancient manor, first mentioned in the Domesday Book but thought to have been built on a holy site possibly dating back to the fifth or sixth century. From 1231 it was owned by the Arundell family, when Sir Remphrey Arundell married Lady Alice Fulcar, heiress of Lanherne, but it did not become their principal residence until 1360. A devout family given to good works, the Arundells remained staunch Catholics after Henry VIII's Reformation in the sixteenth century, and when a party of English Carmelite nuns, fleeing from the French Revolution, was in need of a refuge in 1794, Lord and Lady Arundell gave them Lanherne. It remained an enclosed convent and is now home to the Franciscans of the Immaculate.

The present building dates from Tudor times, with an Elizabethan front, and its former chapel is the Roman

Catholic Parish Church. Though very small, the chapel was lavishly built in the style of Louis XIV, with some highly decorative features. Especially prized by the congregation is the Arundell sanctuary lamp, said never to have been extinguished since pre-Reformation times.

TREYARNON BAY

Treyarnon

Treyarnon Farm

Start/Finish P

Carnevas

Minnows Islands

Will's Rock

Trehemborne

Porthcothan

Walk 14 – Treyarnon Bay

Distance	4.5 miles (7.25km)
Estimated time	2¼ hours
Difficulty	● ● ● ○ ○
Ascent	380ft (116m)
Map	OS Explorer Map 106
Starting point	SW 858741

Notes: A reasonably level walk past a number of headlands and above several coves and islands to the sandy beach at Porthcothan, returning on footpaths through the peaceful farmland behind the coast. Some paths may be muddy, so good footwear is recommended. Dogs should be kept under close control through fields.

From the car park at Treyarnon cross the stream to pick up the South West Coast Path on the far side of the beach, climbing very gently uphill past several headlands and tiny coves. Carrying on past the cluster of offshore rocks at Minnows Islands, follow the Coast Path around Will's Rock and then head inland above the sandy beach to Porthcothan.

Turning left on the road, walk to the junction and turn left again, taking the minor road to Carnevas. Turn right behind new barn conversions at the far end of the campsite to follow the footpath downhill, bearing left through fields to the stream. Crossing the footbridge, continue uphill across the road to the next road. Turn left and go left down the drive to Trehemborne, taking the footpath on the left by the buildings. Cross another stream to turn left on the road beyond and left onto the footpath at the corner, forking right in the third field and heading right in the fields beyond to come out on the road by Treyarnon Farm. Turn right and then left at the junction to return to the car park.

WALK 14

St Constantine's
Church

Harlyn

Start/Finish P

Cataclews Point

Mother Ivey's Bay

Trevose Head

Constantine
Bay

Booby's Bay

Mackerel
Cove

Stinking Cove

Walk 15 – Mother Ivey and St Constantine

Distance	6.25 miles (10km)
Estimated time	2¾ hours
Difficulty	● ● ● ● ○
Ascent	354ft (108m)
Map	OS Explorer Map 106
Starting point	SW 879755

Notes: A long but gentle walk around open ground with big skies and Atlantic sea views, with two picturesque sandy beaches fringed by rocky shorelines and rolling surf, as well as sand dunes, green lanes, an ancient chapel, a lighthouse and a witch's curse!

From the beach car park at Harlyn walk to the road and turn right to pick up the South West Coast Path heading west. Follow it out around Cataclews Point and on around Mother Ivey's Bay, crossing the track to the lifeboat house and continuing around Trevose Head, above Stinking Cove, and Mackerel Cove. After the memorial on your left, the path passes a spectacularly collapsed sea-cave (Round Hole) before dropping gently downhill to Booby's Bay and on to Constantine Bay. Towards the end of the beach turn left on the track through the dunes and left on the road.

Detour left along the far boundary of the golf course to visit St Constantine's Church and Well, otherwise remain on the road to Harlyn. After the road bears sharp right take the footpath left downhill. Turn left on the road after the hamlet to return to the car park.

WALK 15

Booby's Bay.

Mother Ivey is said to have been a sixteenth-century white witch who cursed the family living in the cottage still bearing her name on the eastern side of Trevose Head. According to local folklore, the Hellyers ran a lucrative pilchard business and were one day left with a crate of unsold fish. The people of Padstow had been less fortunate in their fishing and were starving, so Mother Ivey appealed to the Hellyers to donate their surplus stock.

The family refused, instead ploughing the fish into their fields as a fertiliser. Furious, Mother Ivey pledged that every time the soil in that field was broken someone would die. The field was ploughed regardless, and shortly afterwards the Hellyer's eldest son was thrown from his horse and killed. Rumours persisted about the potency of the curse even as late as the 1970s, when a man using a metal detector in the field died of a heart attack, as did the foreman of a water company laying pipes, and the field has been left fallow ever since.

Booby Bay is named after a small white seabird closely related to a gannet, with a yellow head and black wing tips. It is thought that the name derives from the bird's practice of diving offshore in stormy weather.

Just above the beach at Booby's Bay, but not open to the public, is an old fisherman's shelter once made of driftwood, known as 'Tom Parson's hut'.

St Constantine's Well.

Constantine Island, between Constantine Bay and Booby's Bay, hit the national press in 2008, after an amateur archaeologist discovered the remains of a middle-aged man buried 3,500 years ago. The skeleton was interred in a crouched position in a stone cist, an unusual find from a Bronze Age culture that customarily cremated its dead.

Sub-tropical plants thrive in the warm air from the Gulf Stream.

On the other side of the headland, above Harlyn Bay, a field rumoured to be haunted was found to be the site of an ancient cemetery in 1900. Antiquarian Sabine Baring-Gould wrote of more than a hundred graves uncovered, whose boxes of slate contained crouched skeletons, as well as bronze armlets and necklaces of blue and amber glass beads. It is thought that the burials are of many dates from the Bronze Age onwards.

St Constantine of Cornwall, King of Dumnonia in the middle of the sixth century, was allegedly a far from saintly man in his early life. Labelled an 'unclean whelp' by St Gildas, Constantine was accused of disguising himself as a bishop in order to murder his two nephews in the sanctity of a church, although chronicler Geoffrey of Monmouth commented in his defence that they were in fact the treacherous sons of the evil Mordred, who was later to slay King Arthur.

Constantine Bay.

Later in life, however, a deer being pursued by Constantine took shelter in St Petroc's cell (see Walk 17), and the King was so impressed by the saint's holiness that he had himself and his bodyguard converted on the spot to Christianity. Soon afterwards he abdicated his throne in favour of his son and took to the holy life himself, founding the churches at Falmouth and Illogan as well as the one preserved on the Trevose Golf Course.

Sea holly flourishes in the sandy soil.

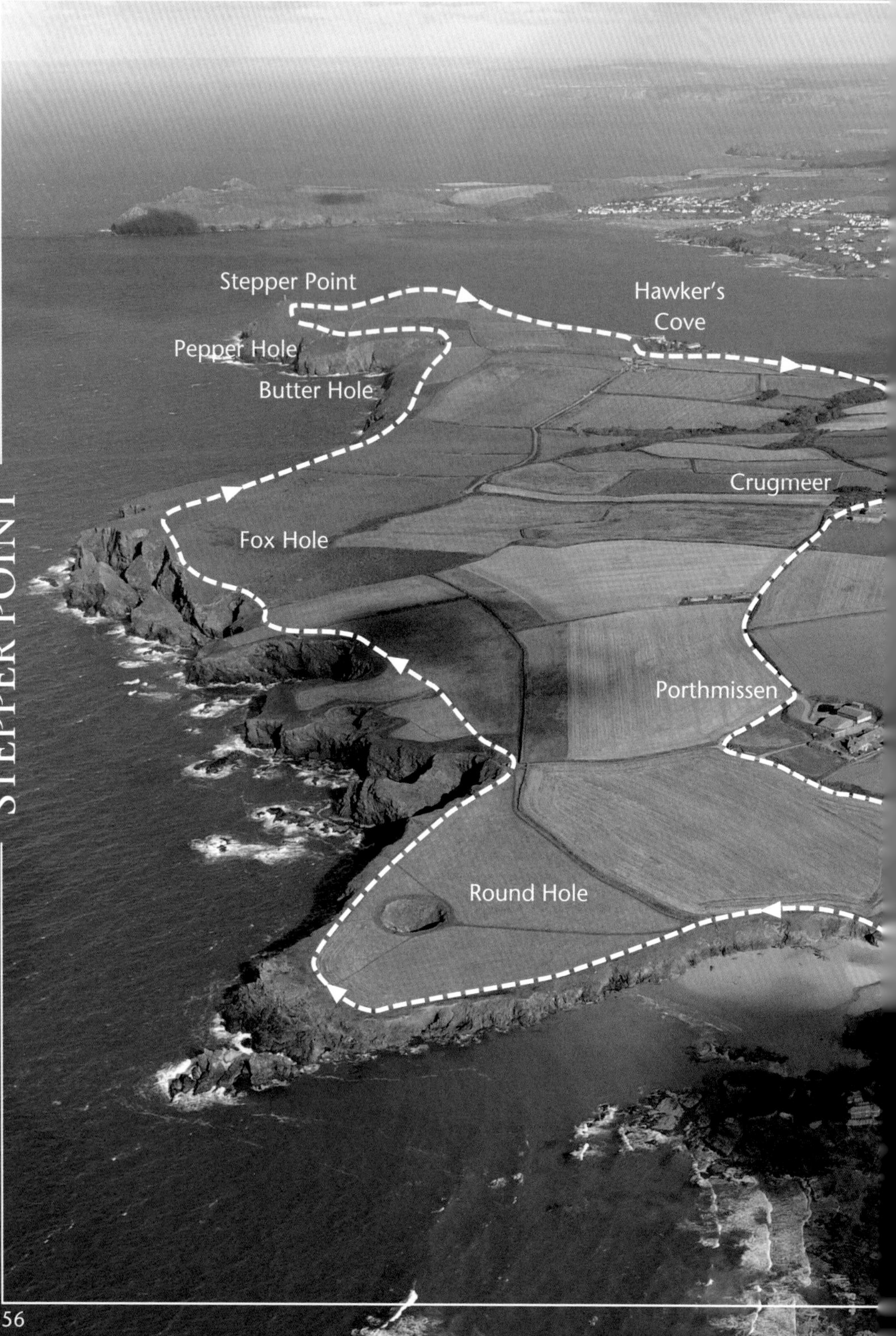

STEPPER POINT

Stepper Point

Pepper Hole

Butter Hole

Hawker's Cove

Crugmeer

Fox Hole

Porthmissen

Round Hole

Harbour Cove

P Start/Finish

Trevone

Walk 16 – Stepper Point

Distance	5.5 miles (8.75km)
Estimated time	2½ hours
Difficulty	● ● ● ○ ○
Ascent	459ft (140m)
Map	OS Explorer Map 106
Starting point	SW 891760

Notes: On the western shores of Stepper Point the pounding waves have eroded the rocks in a spectacular fashion, giving rise to sheer cliffs seamed with vertical chasms and topped with terraces of vegetation where they have slumped.

From the beach car park at Trevone, facing the sea, take the track to the right and follow it around the beach to turn left on the South West Coast Path. Passing the Round Hole, carry on along the coastline, past an old quarry, a disused mine and a number of dramatic rock formations along the cliffs, including collapsed sea caves at Fox Hole, Butter Hole and Pepper Hole. Passing another quarry and a daymark tower, continue around Stepper Point and straight on between the houses above Hawker's Cove.

Above the sandy beach at Harbour Cove turn right on the permissive path before the dunes then left on the road, following it round to Crugmeer. Turn right before the buildings, continuing ahead at Porthmissen to return to Trevone.

STEPPER POINT

Like Bedruthan Steps (see Walk 13), Trevone Bay is a designated SSSI. It has yielded fossils from the Devonian period, which have helped geologists to date this rock-type in the South West. It also contains exposures of an unusual type of basaltic magma, a rock associated with volcanoes, as well as noteworthy limestone formations at Porthmissen bridge, just after Roundhole Point.

Like the dramatic coastline around them, the cliffs between Trevone and Stepper Point have been spectacularly sculpted by the sea's erosion, and as you walk along here you can hear the hollow boom that tells of caves in the rock below your feet (see Walk 5). Several of these caves have collapsed, leaving massive sinkholes. Trevose Head and Stepper Point each have a giant crater in the grass that has been formed in this way, known on each as Round Hole. Pepper Hole, Butter Hole and Fox Hole are smaller examples of the same process.

Pepper was one of the many items attracting prohibitive taxes in the eighteenth and nineteenth centuries, and thus became a popular commodity with smugglers. These sea caves were the perfect hideaway for illegal cargoes, with their rocky entrances and their sandy floors, and pepper and other spices were regularly landed here. In 1765 Padstow resident William Rawlings complained to the Earl of Dartmouth that one day his servants had encountered 60 horses travelling up from a local beach 'having each three bags of tea on them of 56 or 58lbs weight'.

The daymark tower on Stepper Point is thought to have been built early in the nineteenth century, and was originally lime-washed. It was a maritime navigational aid, designed to guide sailors into the River Camel.

The rocky coastline around Padstow has made it hazardous for ships over the centuries, and in 1827 a lifeboat was built by the Padstow Harbour Association. Appropriately named Mariner's Friend, it was stationed at Hawker's Cove. A new boathouse was built there in 1931 for a

Daymark tower at Stepper Point.

Coastal vegetation.

58

second boat. By 1967 both had closed, and a new boathouse with a 240-foot slipway was built at Trevose Head, which it was replaced by the current building in 2006.

In summer the cliffs are topped with thick vegetation, including many wildflowers. The most abundant are ragged clumps of bristly pink-headed thrift, interspersed with patches of vivid yellow mouse-ear hawkweed. A number of edible plants also thrive in the warm, salty air: wild carrot, whose roots can be eaten like their cultivated relatives, dandelion and plaintain, both frequently used in salads, and golden samphire (see Walk 13). The thistles are probably best left for the grazing sheep!

Stacks and gullies

Tregirls
Farm

St George's
Well

P

Start/Finish

Padstow
harbour

Gun Point

Walk 17 – Padstow and the Doom Bar

Distance	2.5 miles (4km)
Estimated time	1¼ hours
Difficulty	● ○ ○ ○ ○
Ascent	190ft (58m)
Map	OS Explorer Map 106
Starting point	SW 918755

Notes: A very gentle stroll through the open ground to the north of Padstow, with far-reaching views down the Camel Estuary to the islands in Padstow Bay. With sandy beaches and dunes full of wildflowers it is a world away from the tourist bustle of the town, and a perfect place for a picnic.

From Padstow harbour take the footpath up the ramp towards the sea, and follow it through the park to the memorial, ignoring the steps up to the left. Pick up the South West Coast Path here and follow it around the shoreline to the beach at St George's Well. The well itself – an unremarkable-looking spring – is in the vegetation at the side of the path.

Continue to the site of Napoleonic gun emplacement and fortifications at Gun Point. Curve inland with the Coast Path as it skirts the dunes, turning left on the track and following it back to Padstow via Tregirls Farm, ignoring the tracks to left and right after you reach the road. Follow Tregirls Lane left onto Church Street, past the Parish Church of St Petroc – the start point of the Saint's Way walking route across Cornwall – and bear right on Duke Street to return to the harbour.

WALK 17

Harbour Cove.

According to a Padstow legend, a mermaid fell in love with a local boy, Tom Yeo. Far from being lured to a watery doom, however, Tom shot the unfortunate creature, claiming that he mistook her for a seal. In her wrath she put a curse on Padstow, swearing that no ships would enter or leave the port for a year. She called up a great sandstorm that swept across the estuary and laid a great sand bar across its entrance – the Doom Bar, still a hazard for sailors today.

Padstow war memorial.

As well as four restaurants in Padstow, top chef Rick Stein has a pub in St Merryn and a chippie in Falmouth. He made his name in the 1990s with a television series based on his life running The Seafood Restaurant in the town. His catch phrase was 'Nothing is more exhilarating than fresh fish simply cooked', and since then he has travelled all over the world in search of culinary inspiration to reproduce in his eateries and in front of television audiences. He has cooked for Elizabeth II and Prince Philip, as well as Tony Blair and former French president Jacques Chirac, and in 2003 he was awarded an OBE for services to West Country tourism.

Over 4,000 years ago, traders and travellers were passing through Padstow from Brittany to Ireland, taking a route overland between here and Fowey to avoid the treacherous waters around Land's End. Today the walking trail known as the Saint's Way recreates the inland route, starting at Padstow's Parish Church.

In the sixth century there was a major influx of Celtic saints into Cornwall. Parts of the Church of St Petroc date back to the twelfth century, but its origins as a holy site date back to the sixth, when the saint arrived in Cornwall and built a small chapel here.

St Petroc was reputedly the son of a Welsh prince who studied theology in Ireland before founding a monastery at Lanwethinoc, which later became Petrocston and then Padstow. The monastery was sacked by Vikings in the tenth century.

Padstow Harbour.

The 'Obby 'Oss

Padstow is internationally renowned for its 'Obby 'Oss May Day celebrations. At midnight the Night Song is sung unaccompanied around the town, and then the town is decorated with the first signs of the summer – bluebells, forget-me-nots, cowslips, hazel catkins and sycamore twigs bursting with new shoots – and the maypole is set up.

At dawn the 'Oss is let out of its stable: a masked man wearing a black cape draped over a huge hoop which he spins mischievously in repeated attempts to trap the young maidens dancing through the town. He is drawn through the streets by a 'teaser' dancing ahead of him, to the accompaniment of drums and accordians. Dressed in white, the townspeople line the streets and sing the Day Song as the procession passes.

There are in fact two 'Osses: the traditional Old 'Oss, and the Blue Ribbon 'Oss, introduced in Victorian times by members of the Temperance Society to express their disapproval of the alcohol consumed during the festivities. Sometimes the two 'Osses dance together at the maypole in the afternoon before retiring to their stables for another year.

Covering 630 miles from Poole to Minehead, the South West Coast Path National Trail leads you through diverse landscapes, all with their own unique story to tell. If the walks in this book have inspired you to find out more about the longest and most popular of the UK's 15 national trails, visit www.southwestcoastpath.com.

Natural England – www.naturalengland.org.uk
Natural England is the government's adviser on the natural environment and provides the majority of the funding for the maintenance of the Coast Path, which is undertaken on a day-to-day basis by Devon County Council and the National Trust. Through Environmental Stewardship Schemes, Natural England also helps farmers and other landowners to protect and enhance the countryside so that nature can thrive.

National Trust – www.nationaltrust.org.uk
The National Trust Countryside Team works seven days a week to restore and care for the characteristic wildlife of the area, as well as working with local communities to improve access and understanding of these special areas. Regular events and opportunities to get involved mean that all ages can help shape their countryside.

South West Coast Path Association – www.southwestcoastpath.org.uk
If you enjoyed these walks, why not join the South West Coast Path Association? This charity represents the users of the trail, campaigns to improve the path and raises money to help it happen. By joining you'll be one of thousands who help to make the South West Coast Path one of the world's greatest walks.

Cornwall Area of Outstanding Natural Beauty – www.cornwall-aonb.gov.uk
The Cornwall AONB makes up approximately a third of the county and is in 12 separate parts. The landscape is diverse and ever changing, cherished by those whose families have worked in it for generations and loved by those who are seeing its beauty and mystery for the first time. It is the essence of Cornwall.

Cornish Mining World Heritage Site – www.cornishmining.org.uk
With an area totalling 20,000 hectares, the Cornish Mining World Heritage Site is the largest World Heritage Site in the UK, and this status places Cornish mining heritage on a par with other international treasures such as the Pyramids of Egypt or the Great Wall of China.

SAFETY
On the beach and coast path

- Stay away from the base of the cliffs and the cliff top and ensure that children and dogs are kept under control.
- Do not climb the cliffs. Rockfalls can happen at any time.
- Beware of mudslides, especially during or after wet weather.
- Always aim to be on the beaches on a falling tide and beware of the incoming tide, especially around headlands. Be sure to check the tide tables.
- Beware of large waves in rough weather, especially on steeply shelving beaches.
- Observe all permanent and temporary warning signs; they advise on hazards and dangers. Check routes beforehand by visiting www.southwestcoastpath.com

- Be very careful on rocky foreshores which often have slippery boulders.
- Stay within your fitness level – some stretches of coast can be strenuous and/or remote.
- Make sure you have the right equipment for the conditions, such as good boots, waterproof clothing and sun screen if appropriate.
- Follow The Countryside Code.

Emergencies
In an emergency dial 999 or 112 and ask for the Coastguard, but be aware that mobile phone coverage in some areas is very limited.